W9-CHE-740

PLAY BALL
BASEBALL

CATCHER

By Jason Glaser

Must Read!

Gareth Stevens
Publishing

Please visit our Web site, www.garethstevens.com. For a free color catalog of all our high-quality books, call toll free 1-800-542-2595 or fax 1-877-542-2596.

Library of Congress Cataloging-in-Publication Data

Glaser, Jason.
Catcher / Jason Glaser.
    p. cm. — (Play ball: baseball)
Includes index.
ISBN 978-1-4339-4484-0 (pbk.)
ISBN978-1-4339-4485-7 (6-pack)
ISBN 978-1-4339-4483-3 (library binding)
1. Catchers (Baseball)—Juvenile literature I. Title.
GV872G57 2011
796.357'23—dc22
                                    2010035720

First Edition

Published in 2011 by
Gareth Stevens Publishing
111 East 14th Street, Suite 349
New York, NY 10003

Copyright © 2011 Gareth Stevens Publishing

Designer: Haley W. Harasymiw
Editor: Greg Roza

Photo credits: Cover, p. 1 Gregory Shamus/Getty Images; cover, back cover, 2–3, 5, 7, 11, 17, 27, 35, 44–45, 46–47, 48 stadium background on all Shutterstock.com; pp. 4, 5 Focus On Sports/Getty Images; p. 6 Chicago History Museum/Getty Images; p. 7 Buyenlarge/ Getty Images; p. 8 Diamond Images/Getty Images; p. 9 Zigy Kaluzny/Workbook Stock/Getty Images; pp. 10, 11, 12 Mark Rucker/Transcendental Graphics/Getty Images; p. 13 Photo File/ MLB Photos/Getty Images; p. 14 Stephen Dunn/Allsport/Getty Images; p. 15 Ken Levine/ Getty Images; pp. 17, 18 Christian Petersen/Getty Images; p. 19 Leon Halip/Getty Images; p. 20 Bruce Kluckhohn/Getty Images; pp. 21, 35, 44, 45 Jim McIsaac/Getty Images; pp. 22, 33 Elsa/Getty Images; p. 23 Ron Vesely/MLB Photos/Getty Images; pp. 24, 37 Greg Flume/ Getty Images; p. 25 Brad Mangin/MLB Photos/Getty Images; p. 26 Scott Cunningham/ Getty Images; p. 27 Kenneth K. Lam/Baltimore Sun/MCT/Getty Images; p. 28 Jed Jacobsohn/ Getty Images; p. 29 Scott Boehm/Getty Images; p. 30 Andy Lyons/Getty Images; p. 31 J. Meric/Getty Images; pp. 32, 38 (Gerald Laird) Harry How/Getty Images; pp. 34, 39 Kevin C. Cox/Getty Images; p. 36 Kevork Djansezian/Getty Images; p. 38 (Kurt Suzuki) Ezra Shaw/ Getty Images; p. 40 Andy Crawford/Dorling Kindersley/Getty Images; p. 41 JupiterImages/ Brand X Pictures; p. 42 Mike Kemp/Getty Images; p. 43 Marc Romanelli/Getty Images.

All rights reserved. No part of this book may be reproduced in any form without permission in writing from the publisher, except by a reviewer.

Printed in the United States of America

CPSIA compliance information: Batch #CW11GS: For further information contact Gareth Stevens, New York, New York at 1-800-542-2595.

CONTENTS

The Man Behind the Mask 4

01: Ever More Dangerous 6

02: All-Time Greats 10

03: Playing Catcher 16

04: Prize Catchers 34

05: Future Star: You! 40

Record Book 44

Glossary 46

For More Information 47

Index 48

Boldface words appear in the glossary.

The Man Behind the Mask

Catchers seem to disappear behind home plate, hunched down and hidden by their equipment. Yet the catcher is usually the one controlling the flow of a game.

Playing from Behind

In the 1968 World Series, the St. Louis Cardinals were in good shape. They led the series three games to one and were ahead 3–2 in Game 5. If they could hold on to beat the Detroit Tigers one more time, they would be the champions.

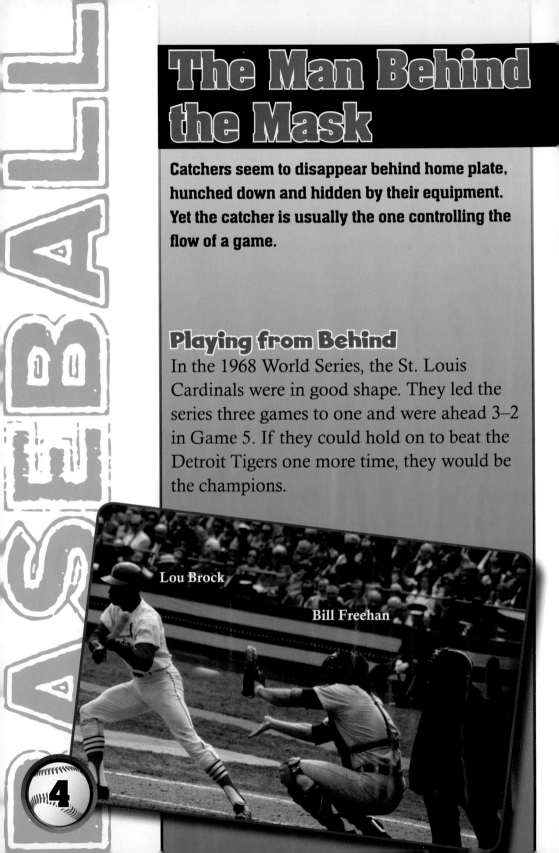

Lou Brock

Bill Freehan

The Cardinals' Lou Brock was on third base when a teammate got a hit. Brock took off from third just as a Tigers player threw the ball to home plate. Catcher Bill Freehan caught the ball and stuck his foot in front of the base, blocking home plate. Brock slammed into Freehan, trying to knock the ball free. Not only did Freehan hold on to the ball for the **out**, he also inspired his team to make a comeback. The Tigers won that game and the next two to become World Series Champions.

Catchers have a physically and mentally demanding job. Read on to learn about the "tough guys" of baseball.

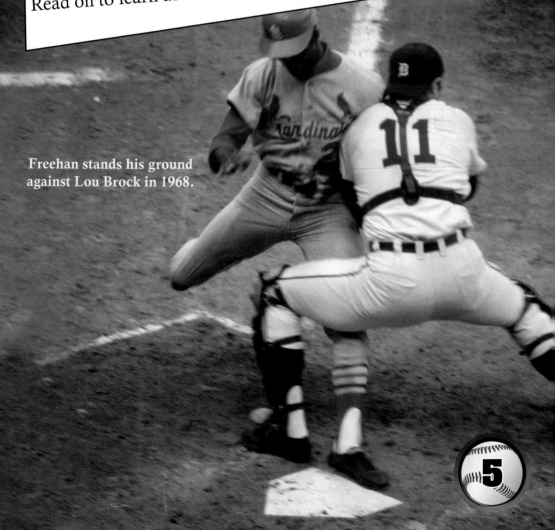

Freehan stands his ground against Lou Brock in 1968.

01 Ever More Dangerous

Baseball was a game first and a sport second. In its earliest days, baseball was played with no gloves, no pads, and no masks. That changed as the sport grew faster and fiercer.

Child's Play

Early bat-and-ball games centered around hitting the ball and not trying to get the hitter out. Pitchers, or "hurlers," were supposed to toss the ball so the batter could hit it. The bare-handed catcher was only needed in case the batter missed or the throw was off.

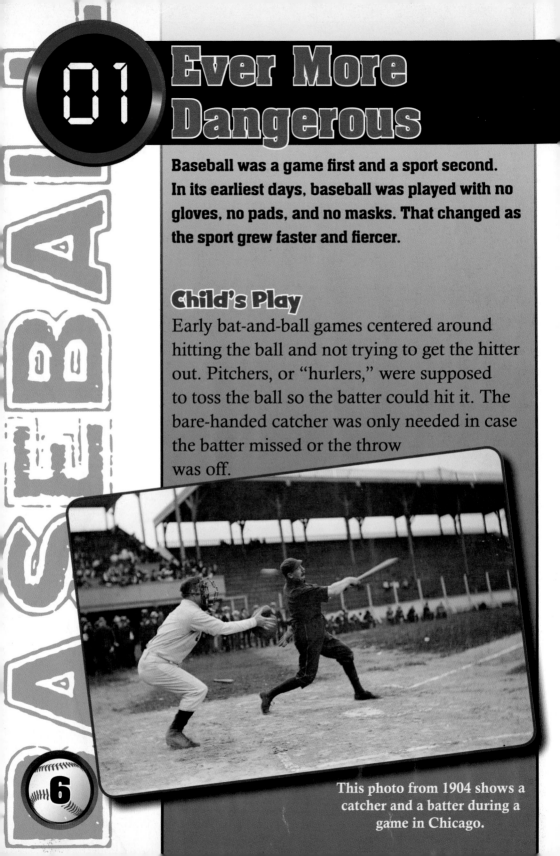

This photo from 1904 shows a catcher and a batter during a game in Chicago.

In the 1870s, star pitcher Albert Spalding began wearing a glove on his catching hand. He also introduced a new kind of baseball and opened his own sporting goods store. He sold baseballs to professional teams. He tried to get players to wear gloves, helmets, masks, and pads. At first, many players thought the gear was silly. However, players soon reasoned that if they got hurt, they wouldn't be able to play—or get paid. Catchers were among the first to wear protective gear because of the danger from the wild, fast pitches being thrown in the early 1900s.

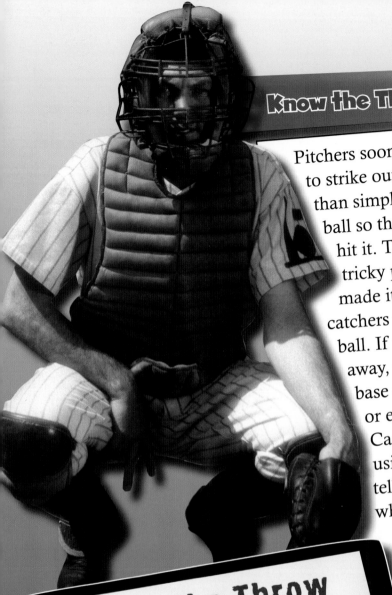

Pitchers soon began trying to strike out batters, rather than simply tossing the ball so the batter could hit it. They developed tricky pitches that made it harder for catchers to react to the ball. If the ball got away, runners on base could advance or even score. Catchers began using signals to tell the pitchers what type of ball they should throw. Catchers also started using larger gloves.

Fixing the Throw

The catcher holds his glove where he expects the ball to cross the plate. He knows what pitch is coming and can tell if the pitch is off. Using a slight pull on the ball as he catches it, a catcher can sometimes make a ball appear to be a strike to the **umpire**. This is called "fixing the throw."

This catcher is using a hand signal to tell the pitcher what type of pitch to throw.

To know what pitches to call, catchers studied the opponent's batters. They identified each batter's weaknesses and what area of the field the batter usually hit the ball to. This allowed catchers to let infield and outfield players know where the hit was likely to go. The combination of pitch calling and position signaling made it easier to get batters out. Catchers had gone from ball retrievers to leaders on the field.

The equipment may have changed, but the skills needed to play catcher have remained the same. Here are some great players who had the skills needed to excel at catcher.

Pioneer at the Plate

A natural athlete, Roger Bresnahan only became a catcher after complaining about the job the current catcher was doing. It was there that Bresnahan helped the New York Giants win a World Series Championship in 1905. Even though the crowds laughed, Bresnahan was the first catcher to wear shin guards in 1907. His experiments with pads and helmets have helped protect generations of players ever since.

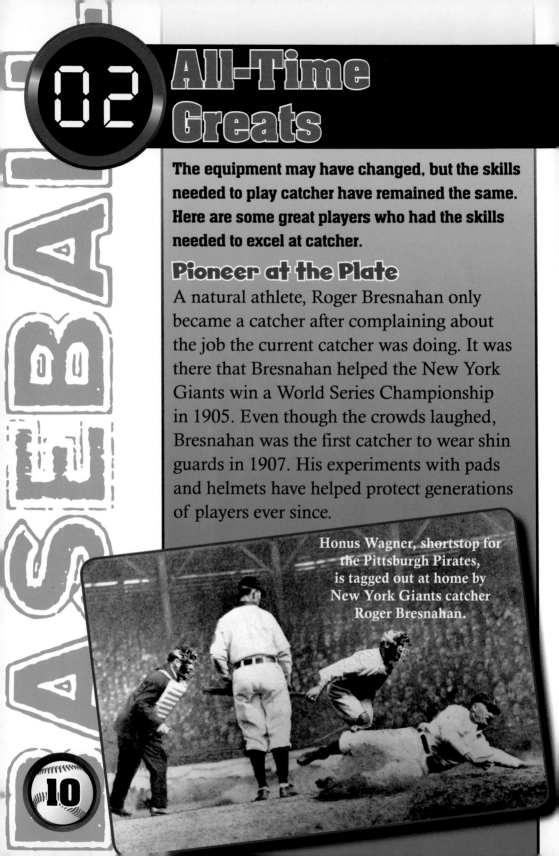

Honus Wagner, shortstop for the Pittsburgh Pirates, is tagged out at home by New York Giants catcher Roger Bresnahan.

Ray Schalk

Fast Hands

During the time Ray Schalk played catcher, from 1912 to 1929, pitchers could do just about anything they wanted to a baseball—which included sanding the ball's surface or spitting on it! The roughed-up spitballs and curves were almost impossible to catch. Not only did Schalk catch those balls, his sure hands recorded the most **putouts** of any catcher for 8 straight years. By not letting wild pitches get past him, Schalk shut down base runners and base stealers every game.

Honest Ray

Eight members of the 1919 Chicago White Sox were banned from baseball for intentionally losing games for money. Ray Schalk is remembered as one of the few White Sox players who refused to take money to lose the 1919 World Series.

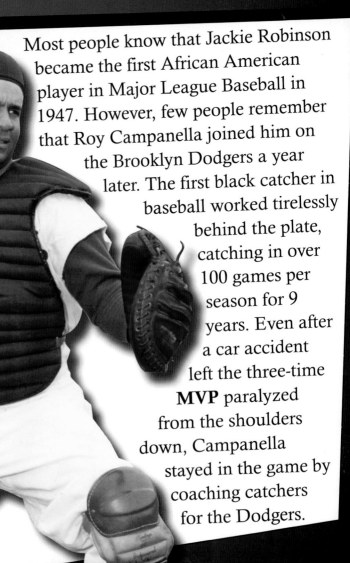

Most people know that Jackie Robinson became the first African American player in Major League Baseball in 1947. However, few people remember that Roy Campanella joined him on the Brooklyn Dodgers a year later. The first black catcher in baseball worked tirelessly behind the plate, catching in over 100 games per season for 9 years. Even after a car accident left the three-time **MVP** paralyzed from the shoulders down, Campanella stayed in the game by coaching catchers for the Dodgers.

In 1942 and 1943, Campanella played professional baseball for the Monterrey Sultans of the Mexican League.

One of the most often quoted people in sports, Lawrence Peter "Yogi" Berra was perhaps the greatest catcher of all time. The lightning-fast, quick-thinking catcher was a key part of the New York Yankees team that won 10 World Series Championships over the course of 18 years (1946–1963). The Hall of Famer was also a three-time MVP and an All-Star for 15 straight years.

Yogi Berra is well known in the sports world for his witty—yet often grammatically incorrect—phrases. He's best known for the phrase, "It ain't over till it's over."

The Little General

Few catchers were as good on **defense** as Johnny Bench. The catcher for the Cincinnati Reds was the 1968 **Rookie** of the Year, a 10-time **Gold Glove** winner, and a two-time National League (NL) MVP. Bench earned the nickname the "Little General" for his ability to direct teammates from behind the plate. His dependable glove and **accurate** throws are still a model for catchers everywhere.

13

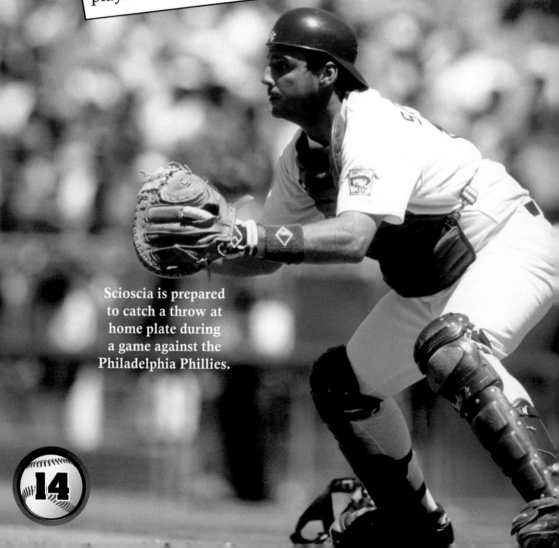

Starting in 1980, Mike Scioscia spent 13 years defending home plate for the Los Angeles Dodgers. Scioscia was willing to stand in harm's way, waiting for a throw to the plate that might not arrive before the runner. His toughness hid an intelligence and understanding of baseball as a whole. Scioscia became the manager for the Los Angeles Angels of Anaheim in 2000. He won two World Series as a player and one as a manager.

Scioscia is prepared to catch a throw at home plate during a game against the Philadelphia Phillies.

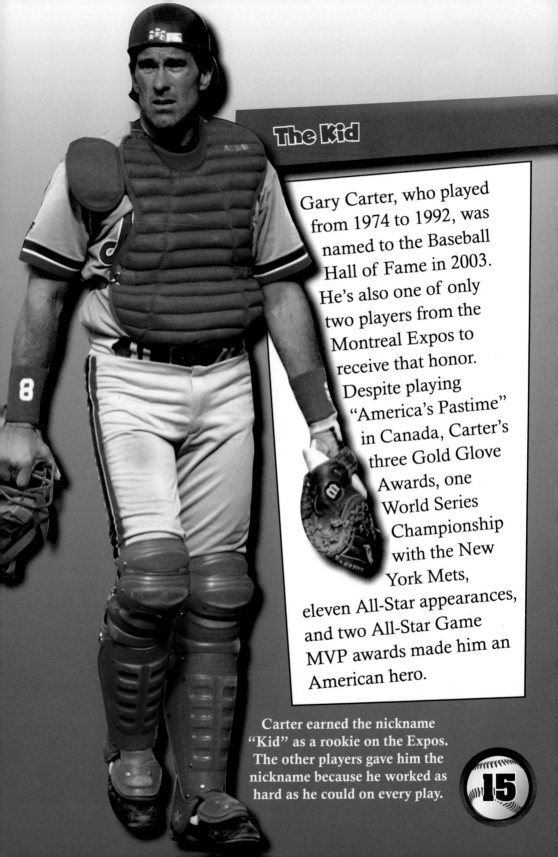

The Kid

Gary Carter, who played from 1974 to 1992, was named to the Baseball Hall of Fame in 2003. He's also one of only two players from the Montreal Expos to receive that honor. Despite playing "America's Pastime" in Canada, Carter's three Gold Glove Awards, one World Series Championship with the New York Mets, eleven All-Star appearances, and two All-Star Game MVP awards made him an American hero.

Carter earned the nickname "Kid" as a rookie on the Expos. The other players gave him the nickname because he worked as hard as he could on every play.

15

03 Playing Catcher

Calling pitches and plays for a whole game is a hard job. Playing catcher takes a strong mind and body. Here is what a catcher goes through.

Behind the Plate

The catcher is the only player who takes his position in **foul territory**. Every ball played begins with a throw to the catcher. The catcher squats behind home plate and faces the pitching mound. He squats down so he can hold his glove near the **strike zone**.

outfield

second base

third base mound first base

home plate

C catcher

Sit and Squat

Catchers place themselves about 2 feet (60 cm) behind the batter so they can catch without interfering with the batter's swing. A usual squat has the catcher balancing on the tips of his toes, leaning slightly forward, knees apart. Some catchers may rest a leg or a knee on the ground, which is easier on their leg joints and muscles. The catcher's glove is the target for the pitcher. The catcher holds his glove where he wants the pitcher to throw. The catcher usually keeps his bare hand behind his back to protect it from wild pitches.

Jason Varitek of the Boston Red Sox prepares for the pitch. Notice that he is hiding his bare hand behind his leg to avoid an injury.

WORKING WITH THE PITCHER

The catcher calls the game, but the pitcher still throws the strikes. A good catcher works with his pitcher to get batters out.

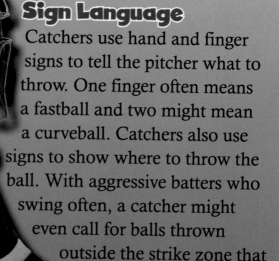

Sign Language

Catchers use hand and finger signs to tell the pitcher what to throw. One finger often means a fastball and two might mean a curveball. Catchers also use signs to show where to throw the ball. With aggressive batters who swing often, a catcher might even call for balls thrown outside the strike zone that the batter might swing at but can't reach.

Cleveland Indians catcher Kelly Shoppach hides his signals to the pitcher so the batter can't see them.

Base runners may try to watch the catcher's signals and give signs of their own to the batter. Knowing the pitch might give the batter an advantage. To keep this from happening, catchers give fake signals, too. Catchers and pitchers work on codes that let them know which signs are real and which are fakes.

Conferences

A catcher is allowed to go out to the pitcher's mound to talk strategy. In tough spots, the catcher might even call in other players to talk over what to do.

Baltimore Orioles catcher Matt Wieters talks strategy with pitcher Kevin Millwood during a game against the Detroit Tigers.

19

At times, a catcher gets pitches he didn't expect. Sometimes, the catcher and pitcher get confused on the signals. Other times, the pitcher loses control of the throw. No matter the reason, the catcher must use his body to stop any ball he can't catch. Catchers use their pads and bodies to keep balls from getting behind them. If they don't, runners on base might advance or score.

Catching Is Important

A dropped ball can give the batter a chance to get to first base. If the catcher drops the third strike in some situations, the batter can try to get to first base even though he should have struck out!

Joe Mauer of the Minnesota Twins must react quickly to snag a wild pitch.

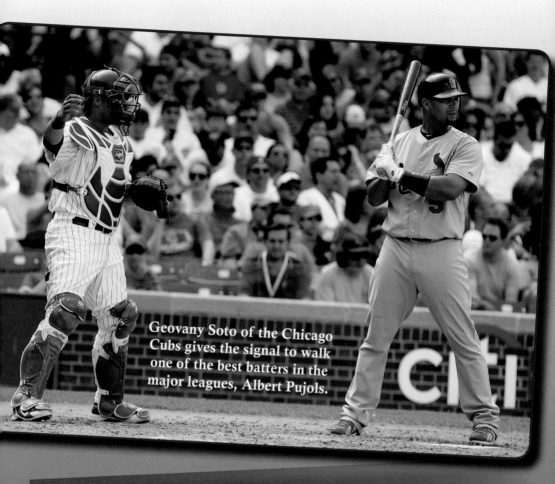

Geovany Soto of the Chicago Cubs gives the signal to walk one of the best batters in the major leagues, Albert Pujols.

Other Calls

A catcher's signals go beyond just the next pitch. He might signal the pitcher to throw out a runner who is **leading off** carelessly. He might have the pitcher throw a pitch way outside the strike zone so the catcher can throw out a runner trying to **steal**. Catchers sometimes call for a pitcher to **walk** a batter on purpose to set up a better chance for an out with the next batter.

DEFENDING THE BATTER

If everything goes perfectly for the catcher, the batter never hits the ball. However, when the batter does get a hit, the catcher may have some work to do.

Bunts and Dribblers

A poorly hit ball may simply roll a few feet in front of home plate. Some batters hit this way on purpose by **bunting**. If a fair ball only rolls a short distance, the catcher must run forward, scoop it up, and make the throw to a base for an out.

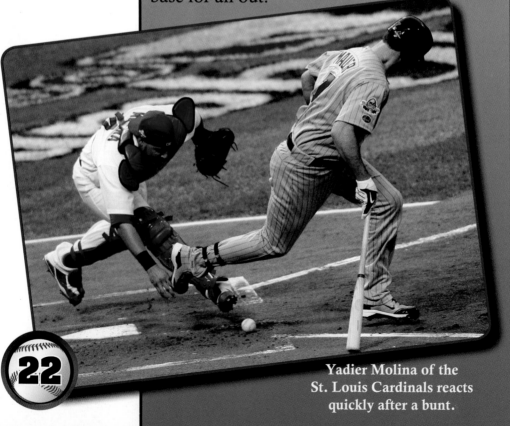

Yadier Molina of the
St. Louis Cardinals reacts
quickly after a bunt.

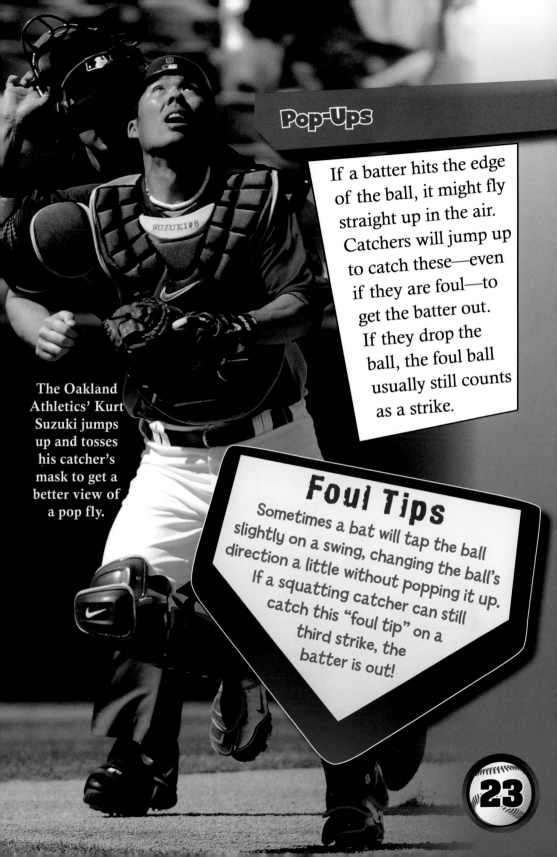

Pop-Ups

If a batter hits the edge of the ball, it might fly straight up in the air. Catchers will jump up to catch these—even if they are foul—to get the batter out. If they drop the ball, the foul ball usually still counts as a strike.

The Oakland Athletics' Kurt Suzuki jumps up and tosses his catcher's mask to get a better view of a pop fly.

Foul Tips

Sometimes a bat will tap the ball slightly on a swing, changing the ball's direction a little without popping it up. If a squatting catcher can still catch this "foul tip" on a third strike, the batter is out!

23

NO STEALING

Throwing out base stealers is another important part of a catcher's job. He must watch the pitcher but also keep an eye on the runners.

Two Seconds to Glory

If a runner on first base takes off during the pitch, the catcher has to catch the ball, stand up, and make the long throw to second base. If a catcher can't receive the ball from the pitcher and get it to the second baseman in under 2 seconds, the runner will probably be safe.

The New York Yankees' Jorge Posada makes a powerful throw to stop the runner from stealing second base.

24

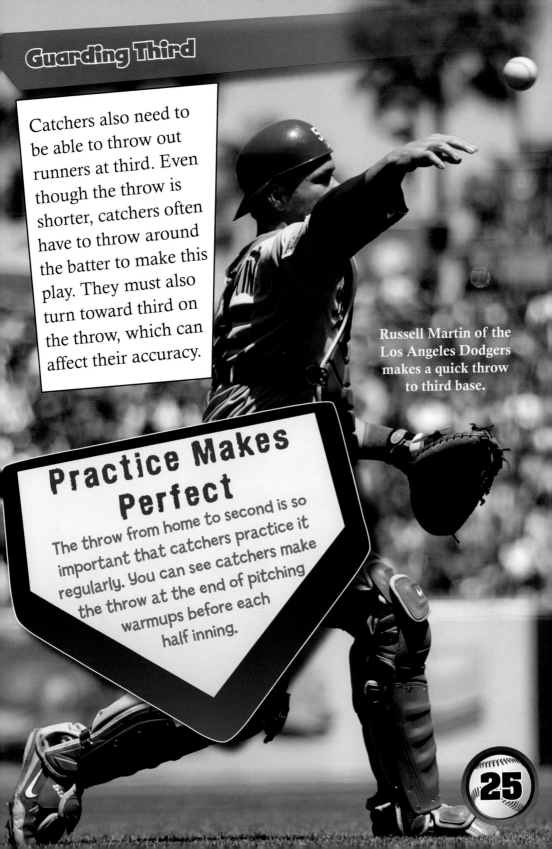

Catchers also need to be able to throw out runners at third. Even though the throw is shorter, catchers often have to throw around the batter to make this play. They must also turn toward third on the throw, which can affect their accuracy.

Russell Martin of the Los Angeles Dodgers makes a quick throw to third base.

Practice Makes Perfect

The throw from home to second is so important that catchers practice it regularly. You can see catchers make the throw at the end of pitching warmups before each half inning.

COMING HOME

Catchers can't interfere with runners, but they can block the path of a runner trying to reach home plate. That means standing between the runner and home plate while waiting to catch the ball.

Tagging the Runner

If a runner runs into a catcher with the ball, the runner's out only if the catcher touches him with the ball or the glove holding it. The catcher crouches in a low, balanced **stance** to catch the ball so he can get his glove down more quickly.

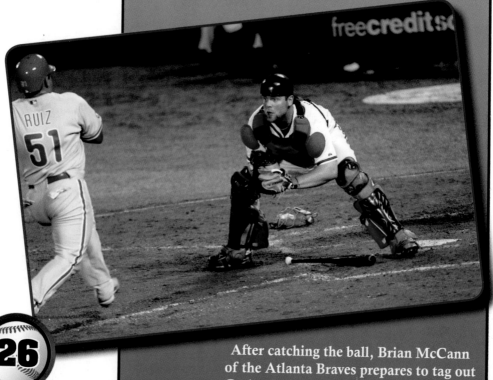

After catching the ball, Brian McCann of the Atlanta Braves prepares to tag out Carlos Ruiz of the Philadelphia Phillies.

Just Right for Right-Handers

There are very few left-handed catchers because of the throw to home. Right-handers can face the field and catch the throw with their glove on the runner's side, closer to the tag.

Catchers don't want to get run over at home plate, but blocking home guarantees getting hit and risking an injury. Catchers are only trying to slow the runner down. Most catchers block only part of the plate, forcing runners to go around them to touch home. That half second delay can be enough for the catcher to get the ball and make the tag.

The Los Angeles Angels' Mike Napoli blocks home plate so Matt Wieters cannot score.

27

KEY SKILLS

Even though the catcher is the team's thinker, he also needs to be in great shape. Here's why.

Flexibility and Strength

A catcher squats for every pitch thrown for the entire game. This might be close to 150 times. The squat position places great strain on the catcher's ankles and the backs of his legs. Catchers work on staying **flexible** so their legs don't get tight or stiff during a game. Catchers must have strong legs so they can spring to their feet over and over.

Staying strong and flexible allows the Boston Red Sox's Victor Martinez to make stunning plays game after game.

Reaction Time

A ball goes from the pitcher's hand to home plate in less than a second. A catcher has to see the ball and react to it in a heartbeat. If he can't, the ball might hit him or get past him. The catcher must also recognize off-target pitches in order to lean or reach as needed without losing his balance and risking a drop.

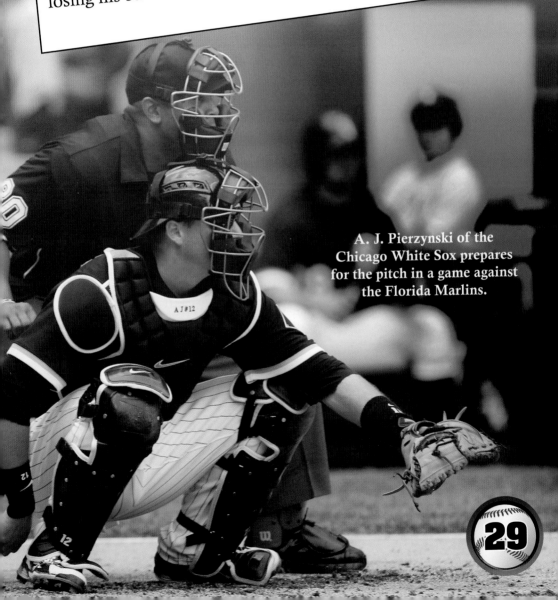

A. J. Pierzynski of the Chicago White Sox prepares for the pitch in a game against the Florida Marlins.

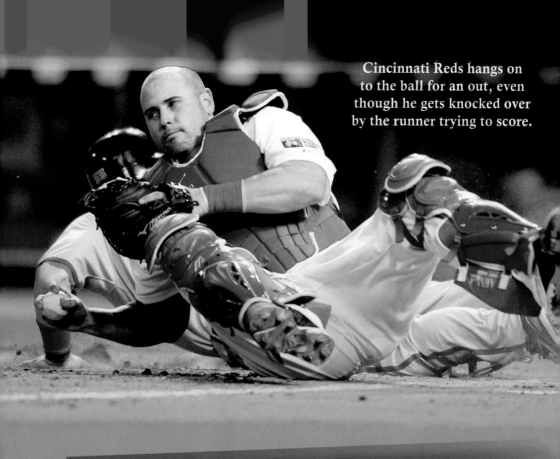

Cincinnati Reds hangs on to the ball for an out, even though he gets knocked over by the runner trying to score.

Courage and Endurance

Even with protective gear, catchers take a pounding. Wild pitches and foul tips can smash into a catcher's head, legs, and arms! Runners sliding into home knock a catcher down or step on his ankles. Catchers can't be scared of baseballs coming in fast or fear getting hurt by runners. They need to stand tall when facing down a runner trying to make it to home plate before the ball. Catchers sometimes take a beating, but they need to get back up and prepare for the next play.

Catchers often do as much throwing as the pitchers. They throw the ball back to the pitcher over and over all game long. Catchers need to keep their arms in good shape to make those throws and still throw out runners on hits. Catchers must also make fast, accurate throws from home all the way to second base on steals. That's among the hardest throws in baseball.

Jason Kendall of the Kansas City Royals throws the ball back to the pitcher after a strike.

BEING PREPARED

A lot of work goes into getting ready for a game. The catcher has to understand the abilities of his pitchers and the other team's hitters.

A Lot on Their Plate

In the pros, teams sometimes play each other several games in a row, and the **lineups** change each game. Catchers may have to study the batting styles of two dozen or more players for each team. They then have to figure out what sorts of pitches have the best chance of getting each batter to miss or hit the ball poorly.

Chris Iannetta of the Colorado Rockies visits the mound to talk strategy with pitcher Jhoulys Chacin.

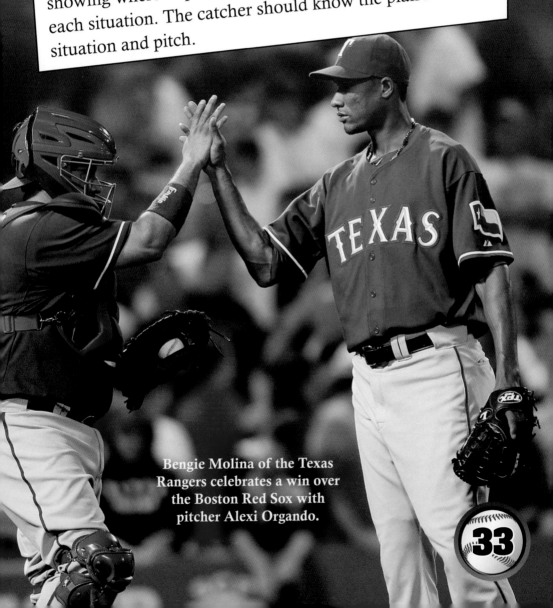

Team Leader

Based on the batter, the runners, and the number of outs, the catcher often decides where the other fielders should play. The catcher knows what pitch is coming and where the ball is likely to go if hit. He can then call the fielders in closer or have them **shift** left or right. Many teams have playbooks showing where to play and how to defend the bases for each situation. The catcher should know the plan for each situation and pitch.

Bengie Molina of the Texas Rangers celebrates a win over the Boston Red Sox with pitcher Alexi Orgando.

Prize Catchers

Catchers are often known as the field generals for their teams. Here are some catchers who could be called five-star generals.

Two Decades Behind the Plate

Since 1991, Ivan Rodriguez has been bringing teams the catching excellence that has made him the active leader for **assists** and putouts among catchers. In nineteen seasons, he's won thirteen Gold Glove Awards—more than any other catcher. Although nearing the end of his career, Rodriguez still runs down grounders, grabs pop flies, and throws out steals like an All-Star.

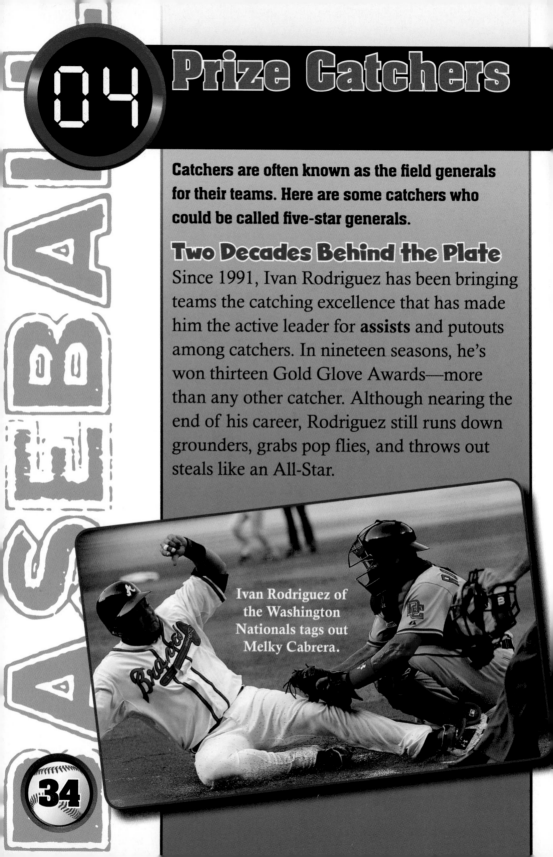

Ivan Rodriguez of the Washington Nationals tags out Melky Cabrera.

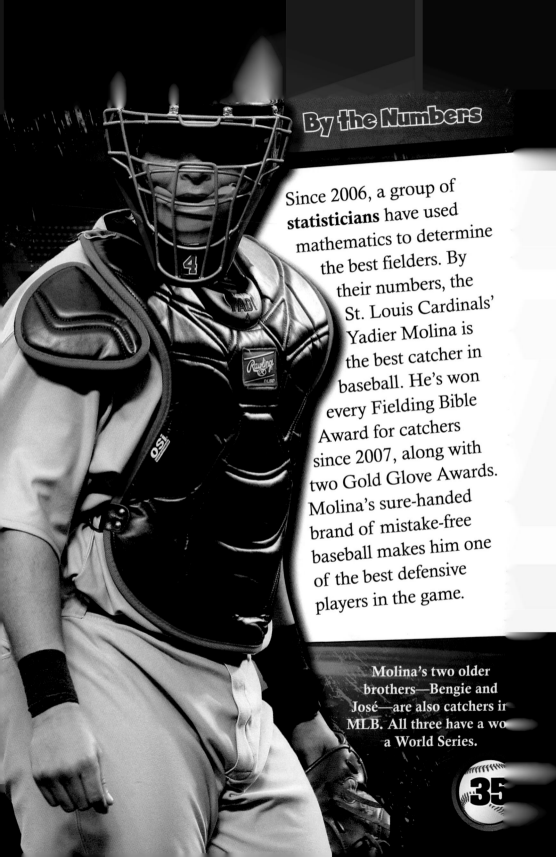

Since 2006, a group of **statisticians** have used mathematics to determine the best fielders. By their numbers, the St. Louis Cardinals' Yadier Molina is the best catcher in baseball. He's won every Fielding Bible Award for catchers since 2007, along with two Gold Glove Awards. Molina's sure-handed brand of mistake-free baseball makes him one of the best defensive players in the game.

Molina's two older brothers—Bengie and José—are also catchers ir MLB. All three have a wo a World Series.

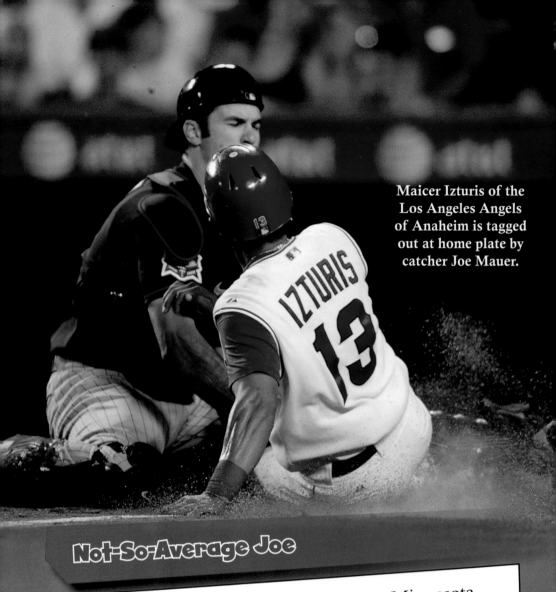

Maicer Izturis of the Los Angeles Angels of Anaheim is tagged out at home plate by catcher Joe Mauer.

Not-So-Average Joe

Many people credit Joe Mauer for the Minnesota Twins' success. One of his strengths is getting good games out of average pitchers against strong opponents. The arm of this two-time Gold Glove winner is good enough to keep runners from trying to steal, and he excels at keeping bad pitches from turning into stolen bases or runs scored.

Teams looking to turn around a decade or more of losing records usually don't celebrate **drafting** a new catcher. The Baltimore Orioles' Matt Wieters is the exception. His knowledge of batters helps his pitchers get wins. His excellent arm can shut down runners on any base, and his steady defense makes him a great fielder. Should the Orioles start winning again, Wieters is sure to be a large part of their success.

Matt Wieters of the Baltimore Orioles catches a pop-up in front of Ty Wigginton.

The Daily Defender

Kurt Suzuki has been a major help to the Oakland Athletics' defense since 2007. Even while putting in more games behind the plate than any other catcher in 2008 and 2009, Suzuki had among the fewest errors. He also led the league in putouts. His everyday endurance gives Oakland a reliable cornerstone on defense day in and day out.

The Tiger's Laird

Stealing bases against the Detroit Tigers doesn't come easily when Gerald Laird is behind the plate. The amazing Tigers catcher threw out more base stealers in 2009 than any other catcher. He also had the best **fielding percentage** for a catcher in the American League (AL).

Jason Varitek has been a leader on the field from Little League to two World Series victories. In 2004, the Gold Glove–winning Red Sox catcher was named the team's captain—only the third player in Red Sox history with that title. His skill with pitchers has been the guiding force behind his participation in four **no-hitter** games, which is a major league record.

Varitek is one of only two players to play in a Little League World Series, a College World Series, and a Major League World Series.

39

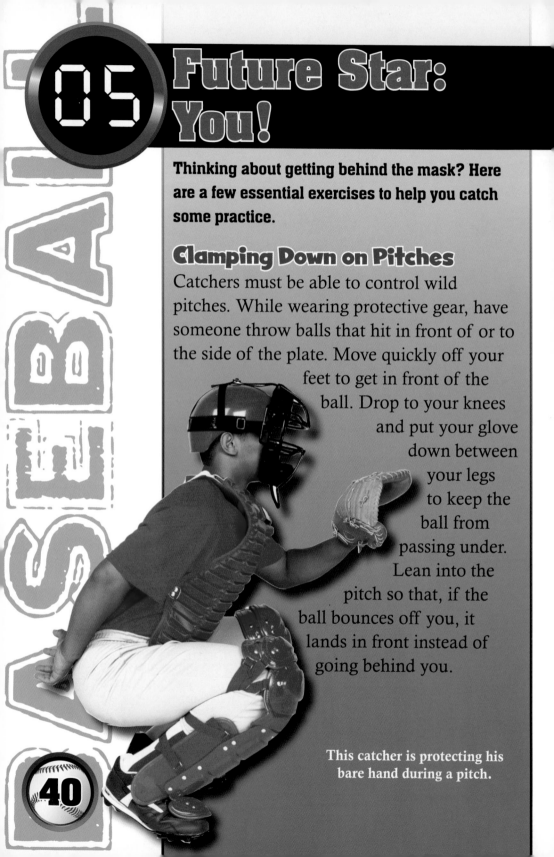

05

Future Star: You!

Thinking about getting behind the mask? Here are a few essential exercises to help you catch some practice.

Clamping Down on Pitches

Catchers must be able to control wild pitches. While wearing protective gear, have someone throw balls that hit in front of or to the side of the plate. Move quickly off your feet to get in front of the ball. Drop to your knees and put your glove down between your legs to keep the ball from passing under. Lean into the pitch so that, if the ball bounces off you, it lands in front instead of going behind you.

This catcher is protecting his bare hand during a pitch.

BASEBALL

Safety First

All catcher exercises should be done in full gear. It keeps you safe and gets you used to moving around in the gear.

Fast Hands

To practice reacting to pitches quickly, have three "pitchers" stand on the mound, each with a bucket of balls. Have the first pitcher throw the ball to you while you are in your stance. As soon as you catch the ball, roll it off to the side and prepare for the next pitcher's throw. See how quickly you can catch and release balls without dropping them.

41

Handling the Pop Up

When going for a pop-up, pull your mask off right away so you can see better but hold on to it. Turn around toward the backstop and look up for the ball. Once you see the ball, throw your mask clear where you won't step on it. Move under the ball and watch it come down into the glove. Use your free hand to trap the ball in the glove so it doesn't fall out.

Catching Flies

A partner can throw balls up from home plate for this exercise. For practicing very high flies, your partner can hit tennis balls straight up with a tennis racket.

Catchers need strong legs and good reflexes to spring up from a squat.

The Dribbler

To practice chasing down bunts or slow-hit "dribblers," get into position behind home plate. Have a partner roll slow balls out from behind you. Quickly pull your mask off and toss it clear. Reach down with both hands to scoop up the ball, since the catcher's mitt makes picking up balls hard. Turn your body and point your shoulder toward first base before making your throw. Your target is the first baseman's glove, which is held wide of the bag so you don't hit the runner on the throw.

43

Record Book

How do the best catchers measure up? The following lists compare top catchers in six key areas.

Highest Career Putouts for a Catcher:

1. Ivan Rodriguez *(still active)* **14,611** *(as of 10/1/10)*
2. Jason Kendall *(still active)* **13,019** *(as of 10/1/10)*
3. Brad Ausmus *(still active)* **12,829** *(as of 10/1/10)*
4. Gary Carter **11,785**
5. Carlton Fisk **11,369**

Chris Snyder

Highest Career Fielding Percentage for a Catcher:

1. Chris Snyder *(still active)* **.9978** *(as of 10/1/10)*
2. Mike Redmond *(still active)* **.9958** *(as of 10/1/10)*
3. Joe Mauer *(still active)* **.9957** *(as of 10/1/10)*
4. Damian Miller **.9952**
5. A. J. Pierzynski *(still active)* **.9949** *(as of 10/1/10)*

Highest Single-Season Fielding Percentage for a Catcher:

Eleven players with 1.000: Spud Davis (1939), Buddy Rosar (1946), Lou Berberet (1957), Pete Daley (1957), Yogi Berra (1958), Rick Cerone (1988), Chris Hoiles (1997), Charles Johnson (1997), Mike Matheny (2003), Chris Iannetta (2008), Chris Snyder (2008)

Highest Career Assists for a Catcher (includes throwing out base stealers):

1. Deacon McGuire   **1,860**   (1884–1912)
2. Ray Schalk   **1,811**   (1912–1929)
3. Steve O'Neill   **1,698**   (1911–1928)
4. Red Dooin   **1,590**   (1902–1916)
5. Chief Zimmer   **1,580**   (1884–1903)

Most Gold Glove Awards by a Catcher:

1. Ivan Rodriguez *(still active)*   13
2. Johnny Bench   10
3. Bob Boone   7
4. Jim Sundberg   6
5. Bill Freehan   5

All-Star Appearances by a Catcher:

1. Yogi Berra   15
2. Johnny Bench   14
   Ivan Rodriguez *(still active)*   14
4. Mike Piazza   12
5. Gary Carter   11
   Bill Dickey   11
   Carlton Fisk   11
   Bill Freehan   11

Ivan Rodriguez

Glossary

accuracy: on target

assist: a throw or contact with the ball that leads to an out. For catchers, catching a third strike is also recorded as an assist

bunt: a soft, directed hit used to advance base runners that does not travel very far from the plate

defense: the team trying to stop the other team from scoring

draft: selecting a player from a pool of potential players entering the league

fielding percentage: a measure of a fielder's ability, determined by adding putouts and assists, and dividing that number by putouts, assists, and errors

flexible: able to bend and move easily without injury

foul territory: the area of the field outside the foul lines. A ball hit into foul territory is said to be "foul."

Gold Glove: an award given each year to the player with the highest fielding percentage at each defensive position in each league

leading off: taking a few steps off the base in order to get a head start running toward the next base

lineup: the active team players for a given game

MVP: most valuable player

no-hitter: a game in which a pitcher goes for the whole game without letting a batter hit safely on to base

out: unsuccessful at getting to the next base without being tagged or otherwise stopped by the defense

putout: causing a batter or runner to become out through one's actions on defense

rookie: a person playing his first year in a league

shift: moving players defensively to adjust for a situation or batter's hitting style

stance: the way a player stands or prepares for a play

statistician: a person who studies and uses numbers and data to analyze and judge players or teams

steal: to advance to the next base successfully without the batter first hitting the ball

strike zone: the imaginary rectangular area over the plate between the batter's knees and armpits that is the pitcher's target

umpire: a field official who judges the events of the game

walk: when a batter receives four balls outside the strike zone while at bat, allowing the batter to take first base.

For More Information

Books

Bowen, Fred. *The Golden Glove*. Atlanta, GA: Peachtree Publishers, 2009.

Buckley, James. *Baseball*. New York, NY: DK Publishing, 2010.

Christopher, Matt. *The Catcher's Mask*. Chicago, IL: Norwood House Press, 2009.

Dreier, David. *Baseball: How It Works*. Mankato, MN: Capstone Press, 2010.

Jacobs, Greg. *The Everything Kids' Baseball Book*. Avon, MA: Adams Media, 2010.

Lupica, Mike. *Safe at Home*. New York, NY: Philomel Books, 2008.

Web Sites

Club MLB
web.clubmlb.com
Major League Baseball's activity-filled site has games and interactive fun features to teach kids about baseball and its past and present players.

Kids Club
mlb.mlb.com / mlb / kids
Major League Baseball's site has information for kids who want to learn more about how to be a better player or want to write to their favorite player. The site also provides links to the pages of each Major League Baseball team.

National Baseball Hall of Fame and Museum
baseballhall.org
The Web site for the National Baseball Hall of Fame and Museum in Cooperstown, New York, tells the in-depth history of the game. Learn about the achievements of some of the finest players and personalities from more than 200 years of baseball.

Publisher's note to educators and parents: Our editors have carefully reviewed these Web sites to ensure that they are suitable for students. Many Web sites change frequently, however, and we cannot guarantee that a site's future contents will continue to meet our high standards of quality and educational value. Be advised that students should be closely supervised whenever they access the Internet.

Index

All-Star 13, 15, 34, 45
assists 34, 45
Ausmus, Brad 44

Bench, Johnny 13, 45
Berberet, Lou 44
Berra, Yogi 13, 44, 45
Boone, Bob 45
Bresnahan, Roger 10

Campanella, Roy 12
Carter, Gary 15, 44, 45
Cerone, Rick 44

Daley, Pete 44
Davis, Spud 44
Dickey, Bill 45
Dooin, Red 45

fielding percentage 38, 44
Fisk, Carlton 44, 45
Freehan, Bill 4, 5, 45

Gold Glove 13, 15, 34,
    35, 36, 39, 45

Hoiles, Chris 44

Iannetta, Chris 32, 44

Johnson, Charles 44

Kendall, Jason 31, 44

Laird, Gerald 38

Matheny, Mike 44
Mauer, Joe 20, 36, 44
McGuire, Deacon 45
Miller, Damian 44
Molina, Yadier 22, 35

O'Neill, Steve 45

Piazza, Mike 45
Pierzynski, A. J. 29, 44
putouts 11, 34, 38, 44

Redmond, Mike 44
Rodriguez, Ivan 34, 44,
    45
Rosar, Buddy 44

Schalk, Ray 11, 45
Scioscia, Mike 14
Snyder, Chris 44
Sundberg, Jim 45
Suzuki, Kurt 23, 38

Varitek, Jason 17, 39

Wieters, Matt 19, 27, 37

Zimmer, Chief 45

About the Author

Jason Glaser is a freelance writer and stay-at-home father living in Mankato, Minnesota. He has written over fifty nonfiction books for children, including books on sports stars such as Jackie Robinson. As a youngster playing youth baseball, he once completed an unassisted triple play, which is the highlight of his sports career.